I0558672

BUILT FROM BROKEN

FROM HOMELESS TO MILLIONAIRE

BY:

CAPRICIA A SLOAN

ACKNOWLEDGEMENT

I would like to express my deepest gratitude to my sister, Santarious Sloan, for always being by my side through every season of life. She has walked with me step by step, never wavering in her support.

To my sister, Demetrrius Andrews, thank you for your prayers and encouragement during my lowest moments.

To my sister, Chameisha Nolley, I am grateful for your help and unwavering support. To my brother, Stanley Duffy, your encouragement has meant the world to me.

To my children — SaVon Turney, Raiana Johnson, and Willie Johnson — thank you for never losing faith in me. In the eyes of a child, a mother is like God, and the love you have shown me has given me the strength to endure.

Finally, I want to thank everyone who has supported me throughout my life's journey.

DEDICATION

I dedicate this book to my mother, whose unshakable
prayers and love have carried me through. She is one of the
strongest women I know, and her strength has been my
guiding light.

PROLOGUE

This book serves as an introduction to the events that have shaped my life. I have faced many challenges, yet through each trial, I found the strength to survive and grow stronger.

These pages reflect not just the hardships I endured, but also the resilience and faith that brought me through. This is my journey, and I share it with you in the hope that it may bring you strength and inspiration.

Table of Contents

CHAPTER 1: BORN BETWEEN THE LINES

"I placed you between worlds so you'd learn how to stand in both — but belong to none."

Some stories begin in a hospital room or a quiet home cradled in love and lullabies. Mine began between two opposing worlds, one humming with sirens and shadows, and the other swaying with pine trees and whispers of peace. I was raised between the city's sharp edges and the countryside's soft hands. That's where I learned to live, between the lines.

Atlanta in the late seventies and early eighties was a city divided. On one end, skyscrapers pierced the sky with ambition; on the other, forgotten neighborhoods told stories in broken glass and sirens. I came of age in those streets, running with one foot in survival and the other in hope. In our part of town, hunger was spiritual. It crept into homes, emptied pantries, and settled into children's bones. You felt it even when your stomach was full.

I was still little when I first felt the weight of danger in the air. Not imagined, but real, chilling, and close. It was the era of the Atlanta Child Murders. Children just like me were disappearing, snatched from neighborhoods like ours. They were never seen again. My mama wouldn't let me or my sister out of her sight, and I understood why.

I'll never forget one day at a local fair. I was small enough to still fit under my mama's arm. We were walking through the crowd when I felt her hand slip. A man appeared, picked me up like I belonged to him, and started walking away. I remember the blur of faces, the thud of my mother's footsteps behind us as she screamed and chased him down. A stranger angel in street clothes stepped in, blocked the man's path, and forced him to hand me back. That man vanished into the crowd. But that moment never left us. From that day on, my mother never blinked when we were with her, not once.

The irony was that my father once trained a man who would later be convicted of some of the Atlanta Child Murders and suspected in many more. We were living right in the heart of it all—University Homes and John Hope. I went to school with some of the children who disappeared. I breathed the same air they did. That fear, that trauma, wrapped itself around us like a fog that never lifted. But life wasn't all fear. There was another place. Another version of childhood. And it waited for me in the countryside, where my grandmother lived. Her home was a sanctuary, a safety, and a healing.

When we left the city and went to stay with Grandma, everything changed. There were no gunshots in the distance, no missing children, no watching your back every time you stepped outside. Instead, there was red clay between my toes and the scent of collard greens cooking on the stove. I could ride my bike freely, play until sunset, and sleep with the windows open without worry.

Grandma's land was sacred ground. She had chickens and gardens, a cornfield that rustled like music in the wind. We didn't have much money, but we had what we needed. The earth fed us, and Grandma made sure we never went without. It was a neighborhood built on kinship, my grandma in one house, her sister next door, and family friends just beyond. A patchwork of protection.

And I was her chosen one. Out of all her grandchildren, she kept me closest. While the others played, I was at her side, learning, watching, and growing. She had a way of seeing right through you, as if she already knew the life you hadn't yet lived. *"You're different,"* she'd say. *"You got something strong in you."*

She made me cook, clean, and help around the house, not to burden me, but to prepare me. Every chore was a lesson. Every fishing trip was a conversation about life, about God, about the weight a Black girl carries in this world, and how to stand tall anyway. She didn't raise me for comfort. She raised me for war, because she knew I'd face it.

That duality, the city that hardened me and the country that healed me, made me who I am.

We moved between low-income housing projects like University Homes and later Martel Homes. Both places taught me grit. They taught me how to stretch food, how to protect my sister, how to keep secrets, and how to dream anyway. I remember looking around at those worn-down buildings and knowing, deep in my spirit, "This is not my final destination."

So, I started working. At thirteen years old, I walked into a Wendy's, lied on the application, and told them I was seventeen. I had older friends who vouched for me and helped me fake a work permit. I wore borrowed confidence and a too-big uniform. I took home paychecks and handed them straight to my mother. She was drowning in debt, and I couldn't watch her sink. That job didn't just pay bills, it paid for my first glimpse of freedom.

Responsibility was never optional. It was stitched into my skin early. I didn't have sleepovers or teenage years like other girls. I had work, struggle, and the aching knowledge that if I didn't show up, we'd all fall.

But through it all, I carried a strange knowing inside me, one I couldn't explain, even if I tried. Since the age of two, I'd been having dreams. Vivid, cinematic dreams that clung to me long after I woke. They were more than just sleep thoughts; they were messages and prophecies. They showed me a life far beyond where I was standing.

By the age of ten, I was calling myself Wonder Woman. Not in a game, but in a declaration. I truly believed I was going to rescue my family from poverty, from pain, from that trap of "just enough." I had an imaginary friend too, a girl who walked with me through every chapter of childhood. She never left my side. Some called it imagination, but I called it survival. She reminded me that I was destined for more.

Even when I couldn't see it, I felt it. In the way I worked. In the way I watched people. In the way I held my head high, even when my shoes had holes in them. I wasn't just a little girl growing up in broken places. I was a warrior born between them.

That's how my life began, caught between fear and faith, danger and destiny. I wasn't supposed to make it out. But I wasn't built to stay broken either.

Pause & Reflect:

How did your environment growing up shape how you see yourself today?

Chapter 2: Stolen Childhood & Unbroken Spirit

"They tried to steal your innocence, but I sealed your spirit with strength they couldn't touch."

The weight of my childhood wasn't just in the places I lived or the hunger I felt; it was in the moments that stole pieces of me, moments that should have broken me but instead forged an unbreakable spirit. By the time I was five, I'd already begun to learn that the world could be cruel, that trust could be a fragile thing, and that survival sometimes meant carrying pain in silence. Yet, through it all, I found a resilience that would bring me forward, a fire that refused to be extinguished.

At five years old, I didn't have the words to describe what was happening to me. The first time I was molested, it was a confusing blur, a violation I couldn't fully grasp. I only knew it felt wrong, like a shadow creeping into a place that should have been safe. My mother tried to explain, her voice was gentle but heavy with worry, teaching me about boundaries and the things no one should do to a child. But the lesson came too late, and the damage was done. By the time I was ten, it happened again, this time at the hands of someone who was supposed to be a protector, a minister, my auntie's husband. He was a man cloaked in the authority of faith, someone my family trusted implicitly. His betrayal cut deeper than I could have imagined.

He'd corner me, his words dripping with manipulation, claiming he was stripping the demons out of me. He said my mother knew that this was the only way to save me. The pain was physical, but the emotional toll was heavier; each act chipped away at my sense of safety and my trust in the world. He forced my younger sister to watch, using her as a witness to his twisted justification, telling her this was what happened when demons lived inside you. I couldn't bear the thought of him turning his attention to her, so I made a choice no child should ever have to make. I let him continue with me to protect her, to shield her from the horrors I endured. It was a sacrifice that broke my heart but strengthened my resolve. I'd do anything to keep her safe.

That man's betrayal didn't just steal my childhood; it shattered my view of trust, especially toward men. He was a minister, a figure of authority, yet he used his power to harm instead of heal. It made me question everyone, even those who were supposed to be safe.

Church, once a place of solace, became a place of suspicion and doubt. I never lost my faith in God, but I couldn't reconcile why He would let me suffer. *"Why me?"* I'd ask, my heart heavy with anger and confusion. Yet, even as I distanced myself from organized religion, I held onto a quiet belief that there was something bigger than the pain I was enduring, something that would guide me through.

The trauma of those years didn't end with the abuse. That same man, with his manipulative hold over my family, was the reason we lost our home. He wormed his way into my mother's and auntie's minds, convincing them to trust him with their money, their faith, and their lives.

My Uncle promised to pay the bills, to take care of us, but he didn't. Instead, he isolated us, turning my mother against our extended family, convincing her they were the enemy. His lies left us homeless, moving from one abandoned office space to another, places he controlled. We were at his mercy, and he wielded that power like a weapon.

I'll never forget the hunger that gnawed at me during those days. One memory stands out, sharp and painful. I was about eight, watching him eat a piece of chicken while my sister and I were left to split a single sandwich. My stomach growled, and I dared to ask, *"Can I have some of your chicken?"* His answer was a cold, hard *"No."* I was so angry, so desperate, that I stormed off and slammed into a wall in frustration.

He ordered my mother and aunt to leave the office, and when they did, he turned his rage on me. He beat me, dragging me from the front room up a set of stairs to a rooftop. He threw me across it, leaving scars and scratches on my legs. Then he held me over the edge, threatening to drop me if I ever defied him again. He bit me hard on my neck, and he locked me in a closet filled with what I thought were bats, their wings fluttering in the dark. He called himself a vampire, and in my terrified child's mind, I believed him. To this day, the sight of bats sends a shiver down me, a reminder of that dark, suffocating room.

When my mother returned, I was curled in a corner, crying, my neck stinging and bleeding. She saw the marks but did nothing, her silence a wound as deep as the physical ones. I learned then that I couldn't always rely on the adults around me to protect me. I had to protect myself. The next day, I planned to tell my teacher to find my grandmother, but he kept me out of school for a week to hide the evidence of his cruelty. When I finally returned to school, I was held back in first grade for missing too many days. But I didn't give up.

I memorized my grandmother's phone number, and when I got the chance, I called her from school. She came for me and my sister, taking us to her home in Jonesboro, Georgia. We were skin and bones by then, starved of food and safety, but Grandmother's love was a magic. She refused to let my mother take us back, not until things were stable.

But stability was fleeting. In third or fourth grade, my mother showed up at school without warning, pulling me and my sister out and moving us to East Point, Georgia. She enrolled us in a new school, and we were back in the city's chaos, adapting to yet another upheaval.

When Grandmother realized we were gone, she feared we'd been kidnapped. She searched for us, and I called her again, desperate to escape the cycle of fear and control. Eventually, my mother found an apartment, a small step toward stability, but the scars, physical and emotional, remained with us.

Even in those dark times, I was given responsibilities no child should bear. At seven, I was reading mail for the adults in my life, deciphering words I barely understood. I learned to write checks, filling in the amounts while they signed. It was very tough; I was still learning to read myself, but I had no choice. I'd ask my teachers or older cousins what certain words meant, piecing together the meaning so I could explain it to my family. It was a heavy burden, being the voice and mind for adults when I was still a child, but it taught me to learn fast, to adapt, and to survive.

What kept me resilient through it all was the fight in me, a spark that refused to die. My older cousin was a lifeline, offering guidance and support when I felt lost. But more than that, it was my spirit, the part of me that knew I was meant for more than pain and struggle.

I'd always had that fire, the same one that made me dream of being Wonder Woman, of saving my family from hardship. Even when the world tried to break me, I held onto that vision, that belief that I could rise above. My childhood was stolen in so many ways, but my spirit remained unbroken, evidence of the strength I didn't know I had until I needed it most.

Pause & Reflect:

What painful memory have you carried silently, and how might naming it begin your healing?

CHAPTER 3: BLACK & WHITE WORLDS

"You were never meant to blend in — you were born to stand out between the lines."

The world I grew up in was between the starkly different realities of race, culture, and belonging. Moving from the predominantly white school in Jonesboro, Georgia, to the predominantly Black school in East Point was like stepping across an invisible divide. Each side carrying its own rules, expectations, and challenges.

As a child caught between these worlds, I learned to navigate the complexities of identity, to adapt to environments that demanded different versions of myself, and to find strength in the face of adversity.

In Jonesboro, at the white school, I was one of a handful of Black kids in a sea of white faces. My classroom often had no more than two or three Black students, and the entire school might have had 50 Black kids at most. It was a calm environment on the surface, no fights, no chaos in the hallways, but beneath that calm lay a subtle, pervasive tension. Racism wasn't always loud; sometimes it was in the way teachers overlooked me, or in the fact that we couldn't take Martin Luther King Jr. Day as a holiday.

Walking home was its own gauntlet. Older white kids would drive by, hurling stones or slurs, forcing us to stick to our side of the street. The white side was off-limits, an unspoken rule we learned early. I spoke differently then, proper, polished, almost like a little white girl, as some would later tease. It wasn't intentional; it was just the way I adapted to fit in, to survive in a place where I was always the outsider.

But survival in Jonesboro didn't mean belonging. I was acutely aware of my Blackness, of how it set me apart. Yet, I found a small pocket of acceptance in a white friend who became my anchor. Her name was Sarah, and to this day, we still follow each other on social media, a quiet nod to a friendship that defied the boundaries of our world.

Sarah's parents weren't like the others; they welcomed me, and in her company, I could be myself without fear of judgment. She was a reminder that connection could transcend race, even in a place where differences were so sharply felt.

Then came the move to East Point, to a school where nearly everyone was Black. It was a culture shock that hit me like a wave. Gone was the quiet order of Jonesboro; here, the energy was raw, vibrant, and sometimes overwhelming. The rules were different, the expectations sharper. It was about proving yourself.

Fashion was currency: the right shoes, the right clothes, and the right look. If you didn't have them, you were a mark. Kids would pick at you, tease you, or worse, try to take what little you had. I'd grown up in the projects, so I was no stranger to struggle, but this was a new kind of pressure. I had to learn to carry myself differently, to toughen up, to defend myself in ways I never had to in Jonesboro.

The harassment was relentless. Walking home from the Black school, I faced a gauntlet of boys who'd chase me, trying to touch me inappropriately, my butt, my chest, things no child should endure. It was a stark contrast to Jonesboro, where I could walk home in peace, unbothered by such violations.

The Black school demanded a toughness I hadn't yet mastered, a street-savvy edge that felt foreign after the relative calm of the white school. I had to adapt, to blend in, to learn the unspoken codes of survival. It wasn't easy. There were days I longed to return to my grandmother's house in Jonesboro, where I could run free without fear of harassment. But my mother wasn't letting us go back, so I had to find my place in this new world.

Navigating these two worlds, Black and white, rural and urban meant constantly reshaping my identity. In Jonesboro, I was the proper Black girl, softening my edges to fit in. In East Point, I had to toughen up, adopting a harder exterior to ward off the teasing and the threats. I had friends in both worlds, but belonging was always just out of reach.

In the white school, I was too Black; in the Black school, I wasn't Black enough, my speech and demeanour marking me as different. Yet, I found ways to connect. In Jonesboro, it was Sarah. In East Point, it was a small circle of friends who became my lifeline, older girls who took me under their wing, who showed me how to carry myself with confidence.

One of those girls was like an older sister to me. She lived in the projects, a few years ahead of me in school, and she was on a path out of our circumstances. I looked up to her, followed her, and learned from her. She was graduating from high school when I was still in middle school, and her ambition inspired me.

Another friend, a bandmate from camp, was a few grades ahead, and we'd spend hours together, dreaming of a life beyond the projects. These connections gave me hope, a glimpse of what was possible. They were proof that I could escape the cycle of poverty and pain, that I could build a future on my terms.

In the housing projects, survival meant staying guarded. We didn't go outside much, not until I was about 14. The projects were a world of their own, where danger lurked around every corner, drive-by, fights, and the constant threat of violence.

My coping mechanism was to find people who were going somewhere, who had a vision for something better. I clung to those friendships, letting them guide me. I learned to blend in, to adopt the swagger and style of the projects without losing the core of who I was. It was a complementary act, but it kept me stranded.

The trauma I carried from my earlier years, the molestation, the homelessness, the betrayal, didn't fully register as not normal until I started hearing other people's stories. It was around this time, in my early teens, that I began to piece it together. Listening to my mother's conversations, I realized that what had happened to me wasn't something every child endured.

The man who'd abused me, my auntie's husband, was supposed to be a protector, a father figure, yet he'd caused so much pain. I started questioning why my mother kept him around, why she believed his lies about magic and demons. The weight of it all became too much to handle, and I reached a breach point. I didn't want to live anymore like this.

One day, I couldn't hold it in any longer. I told my mother everything, how he'd molested me, how he'd threatened to kill her if I spoke out. She broke down in tears, spilling down her face, while she said she didn't know. She'd thought he was teaching me to pray, to be godly, when all along he was using his authority to harm me.

My mother confronted him, told him never to come back, but the damage was done. I started seeing a counsellor, someone who helped me process the pain, the anger, and the betrayal. It was the first time I'd spoken openly about what had happened, and it was both terrifying and liberating.

Years later, after I'd had my first child in 1995, the trauma resurfaced in a way I didn't expect. I had a mental breakdown, the weight of those years crashing down on me. I confided in my auntie, the one married to my abuser, and she was devastated. *"I always felt something was mistaken,"* she said, her voice trembling. *"If I'd known, I would've protected you."*

My older cousin, who'd always promised to keep me safe, was furious. He'd never trusted that man, knew he'd caused chaos in our family. Tragically, just days after I told him, my cousin was killed, the first homicide reported in Atlanta in 1996. Then, on the day we were preparing to bury him, my abuser died suddenly.

The doctors couldn't explain it, ruling it a natural cause, but a woman in a store, a stranger, approached my auntie with a message. She said a spirit had taken his soul, that he could no longer harm us. Later, another woman, a Caucasian lady, told me he was sorry, begging for forgiveness from beyond. I didn't know what to make of it, but it felt like closure, like the universe had finally set things right.

Those years, caught between Black and white worlds, taught me to be adaptable, to find strength in the face of rejection and pain. I learned to carve out my own space, to hold onto the people who saw me for me, and to keep moving forward, no matter how heavy the past.

My identity wasn't just Black or white, city or country, it was the resilience I built from living in both, from surviving the worst and still daring to dream of the best.

Pause & Reflect:

When did you first realize you didn't fully "fit in" — and how did you respond to that moment?

CHAPTER 4: LOVE BEFORE KNOWING MYSELF

"Child, don't mistake broken people for mirrors. Let Me show you who you are."

I thought I was searching for love. But really, I was searching for something I had never even felt, so how could I recognize it when I found it?

Growing up without my father's love left a space in me so empty, it rebounded. He was there technically, but his presence never reached my heart. I remember watching other little girls get scooped up by their daddies, kissed on the forehead, told they were beautiful. I waited for that. I hoped for it. But it never came.

So, I did what many broken girls do: I started looking for that love in the arms of men. Not because I was fast or naive, but because I had been taught, almost conditioned, that a woman's worth was somehow tied to having a man. You weren't whole unless you had someone to protect you, to provide for you, and to complete you. That's what I was told. That's what I believed. That's why I chased the idea of love before I ever understood myself.

When I became a mother at seventeen, something in me shifted instantly. Suddenly, life wasn't just about me and my longing. It was about my child, my son, this tiny, beautiful soul who depended on me for everything. I didn't have the luxury of being lost anymore. I had to find my way, even if I had to crawl out of hell to do it.

I made a silent vow the day I held him in my arms for the first time: *"You will never feel what I felt. You will never go through what I went through."* That promise became my mission.

I knew I had to get out of the toxic environment I was in before my son formed memories, before dysfunction became his foundation. And I fought hard to make that happen. I didn't have the tools, the guidance, or the plan. But I had fire in my spirit, and a deep-rooted refusal to let my child become another victim of generational pain.

Looking back, I realize that motherhood saved me in a way. It woke me up. It gave me purpose. It gave me strength I didn't know I had. But it also forced me to grow up before I even knew who I was.

Love, to me, always came dressed as abandonment. It would whisper sweet promises, draw me in close, and then disappear, just like my father did.

After my dad left me emotionally, I started repeating that pattern with men. One after another, they'd enter my life like saviors and exit like shadows. At first, the pain was sharp, shocking, like ripping open a wound that never had the chance to heal. But over time, I grew numb. The abandonment no longer surprised me; it became expected.

I taught myself to stop crying over breakups. To stop begging people to stay. I built a wall so high around my heart that even I couldn't climb it.

But numbing yourself has a price. When you shut out pain, you also shut out the possibility of real love and real healing. And before I knew it, I was carrying my childhood trauma into my adulthood, dragging it into every relationship like a ghost I couldn't shake.

I began to think maybe I was the problem. Maybe I was too broken to love. Too hardened to be held. But the truth is, I just hadn't learned how to love myself.

There came a time when I lowered my standards—not because I didn't know what I deserved, but because I got tired. Tired of being alone. Tired of starting over. Tired of hoping.

And I settled for someone who checked the boxes, but couldn't carry my spirit. He didn't understand the weight I carried or the battles I'd fought. He didn't protect me. He didn't provide for me. He didn't lighten my load. Instead, I became the everything, mother, provider, nurturer, cleaner, and peacemaker. I was doing it all while feeling emotionally starved.

The worst part was that I started convincing myself that maybe this was all I could expect from love. Maybe this was as good as it gets.

But deep down, I knew. I knew that I had become so used to carrying the weight that I forgot I deserved someone who would help me hold it. Someone who would bring peace, not chaos. Strength, not weakness. Presence, not just proximity.

After my first real heartbreak, the kind that leaves you gasping for air in the middle of the night. I made myself a promise that I still hold onto to this day: *"**Never again.**"*

"Never again would I cry over someone who didn't value me."

"Never again would I love someone more than I loved myself."

"Never again would I give someone the power to destroy me."

From that point forward, I decided that my love had to be earned, not assumed. My energy would be sacred. My peace would be non-negotiable. And if a man couldn't love me better than I loved myself, he had no place beside me.

I learned the hard way that you can't pour from an empty cup. Loving someone else before knowing yourself is like building a house on sand; eventually, it will crumble.

What I was seeking all those years wasn't a man, it was validation. It was healing. It was a sense of being seen, valued, and worthy. But no man could give me that. That kind of wholeness only comes from within.

The little girl inside me had to stop chasing unavailable men and start chasing her healing. She had to stop trying to fix others and start fixing herself. She had to learn that her worth didn't come from being chosen, but from choosing herself.

Even now, I'm still healing, unlearning the lies, and still finding softness where I once built stone. Sometimes I catch myself slipping into old habits, craving love from people who can't give it. But then I remember the promise. I remember the little girl who waited for her daddy's love and never got it, and I refuse to let that girl be disappointed again.

I'm not bitter, but I am wiser. I'm not cold, but I am cautious. I'm not heartless, but I finally put myself at the center of my heart.

I now understand that the kind of love I need can't be chased; it must be attracted. And to attract real love, I must first be real love, to myself, for myself, and by myself.

That's what love, before knowing myself, taught me.

And that's why now, I'll never forget who I am just to be loved by someone else.

Pause & Reflect:

Have you ever confused love with validation? What do you now know that you didn't then?

Chapter 5: Marrying the Deception

"Even in the false fairytale, I was whispering the truth — waiting for you to hear me".

When I first met him, I wasn't looking for forever; I was just looking for an escape. He was hanging around the hood, in a rough area, and to be honest, I assumed he was just another street dude. But something about him made me stop and pay attention.

He stood a little straighter. He spoke a little clearly. And as we talked more, I realized he wasn't really from where he was standing. He had college on his mind and business in his heart. He was studying accounting, had big plans, and talked like he knew how to get somewhere in life. That pulled me in.

I wasn't drawn to his looks or his charm as much as I was to what I thought he represented: elevation. A man who could pull me out of my current situation faster than I could do it myself. And in a way, he did. He exposed me to things I had never experienced before. Fancy restaurants. Flights out of town. Vacations that felt like dreams. He took me outside the city limits, literally and emotionally. I remember thinking, *"This is what it feels like to be cared for."* It wasn't just romance, it was escape. And at that point in my life, that was enough.

He introduced me to a new world, but eventually, I realized that just because someone opens a door for you doesn't mean they want you to walk through it for free. Sometimes they open it so they can keep you there, trapped, grateful, and dependent. And that's where the deception began.

What looked like love was layered in manipulation. What felt like support became control. Emotional abuse is a quiet killer. It doesn't bruise your skin, it bruises your spirit. He never laid hands on me, but his words did damage that I still carry today. It was like he knew exactly how to make me doubt myself without ever raising his voice. He'd tell me he didn't mean it, but I knew the message behind the words. One day, I found a message he'd sent to another woman, telling her that I was raised by welfare queens. That my mother, grandmother, and great-grandmother were all on government assistance. That I had a welfare mentality.

He didn't just lie, he rewrote my history like it was a story he could shape to fit his agenda. My family was never on welfare. My grandmother worked her fingers to the bone to provide, even after losing her husband, who had fought in the war. My grandfather served in Vietnam, survived both wars, and came home only to be poisoned and die on American soil. My family had pride, integrity, and grit. But to him, my truth didn't matter, only the version he could spin to make himself look like he rescued me.

And maybe I let him. Maybe, in some ways, I needed saving so badly that I ignored the signs. I wanted the fairy tale so bad that I overlooked the monster hiding in the prince's clothing.

The worst part wasn't what he said, it was what I started to believe. Slowly, I began changing to fit what he thought I should be. I stopped dressing the way I liked. I stopped doing the things I loved. If something reminded him of the projects or felt too cover, he dismissed it, and I dismissed myself right along with it. I was no longer living for myself, I was performing for him. Trying to be the polished, Spelman-type woman he claimed he wanted, when all I ever was... was me. And it should've been enough.

There were days I couldn't even recognize myself. Everything I did went through his filter and his judgment. And even when I had good ideas, he'd find a way to take control or shut them down. I slowly became his project. And the more I tried to shine, the more he dimmed the light.

But betrayal doesn't always come in one blow, it builds. He started cheating. At first, I was devastated. Then I got angry. I had grown up thinking that if a man stepped out, you stepped out too. If he hurt you, you hurt him back. That was the code. So, I did. I found someone who made me feel seen again. Someone who reminded me I was still desirable, still worthy. But all it did was create more confusion, more hurt.

He told me during counselling that he never really wanted to be married in the first place. Said he wasn't ready. That he just wanted a break from the kids and the responsibilities. He said when he got married, suddenly women were throwing themselves at him, not because they wanted to build with him, but because they saw the ring as a sign of security, a chance to get what they wanted without commitment. He got caught up in the attention, the fantasy. And somewhere along the way, he convinced himself that those women were better than me for him.

Ironic, isn't it? He clipped my wings, then blamed me for not flying. He thought he was trading up, but he never even gave me the chance to evolve. Every time I tried to better myself, he stood in the way. He didn't want me to grow, he wanted me to stay small, manageable, and dependent.

I was still loyal, though. I had children with this man. A home. A life. I was fighting for something real while he was out playing with illusions. I couldn't just walk away, not then. I wasn't ready to let go of the picture I painted in my mind. I kept telling myself, *"This is just a phase, this is marriage, this is what commitment looks like."* But in reality, I was married to an idea that didn't exist. A man who wore love like a costume, only to rip it off when the lights went down.

It's hard to admit that I lost myself. That I gave someone the drawing of my soul and trusted him not to destroy it. But he did. Little by little, until I woke up one day and didn't even know who I was.

I stayed too long. Not because I was weak, but because I wanted to believe. I wanted to believe that the man who once flew me across the country and opened my world could also be the man who respected, honoured, and loved me. But the truth is, he was never that man. He was a lesson wrapped in charm, a taker disguised as a giver.

And me? I was just a woman who married the deception.

But even in that, I learned. I learned the difference between being loved and being used. I learned that validation can't come from someone who doesn't value you. I learned that you can survive heartbreak, but losing yourself is far more dangerous. And most importantly, I learned that healing only begins when you finally decide to stop chasing the version of love that almost killed you.

Now, I no longer measure love by gifts, trips, or appearances. I measure it by peace. By how I feel when I'm with someone. Safe? Free? Myself? That's love. Everything else is just decoration.

I left the marriage with scars, but also with strength. He may have taught me some things, but I taught myself how to come back. And that's a lesson no one can ever take away from me.

Pause & Reflect:

What "perfect picture" did you once chase that turned out to be a mask?

CHAPTER 6: WHEN LOVE TURNED DEADLY

"I let your fear grow loud — so My whisper could become your lifeline."

Some kinds of love make you feel alive, like the sun finally broke through after a long stretch of storm. But there are other kinds, the dangerous kinds that wrap around your neck like silk and squeeze like rope. That's what it felt like with him. With RG.

It started so simply, so innocently. A conversation over watches in my boutique. He loved his timepieces, gold, silver, and leather bands. He was clean, smooth, and well-dressed, and he carried himself like a man who had something. I'd seen him come into the shop a few times, but one day he came in while I was working instead of my husband. That's when it shifted.

We talked about the watches, about fashion, and about life. I told him I usually wasn't there during those hours; my husband ran the shop then. But that day, I was there. I used to believe that timing was everything, and looking back, I still believe it, but not always in a good way.

He asked me out after a few visits, and I said yes. Not because I was looking for anything, I wasn't. I had a baby and was trying to lose the weight. Trying to feel like myself again. At that time, my husband didn't even look at me. He didn't acknowledge the effort I was making to love myself again. He didn't see that I was trying to rise. But RG did. He saw me.

We started going to the gym together. Started sharing workouts, water bottles, sweat, and laughs. And when you've been ignored for so long, attention starts to feel like affection. And affection starts to feel like love. And love, at least the kind I thought I was getting, felt like a reason to breathe again.

The affair happened gradually, then all at once. I didn't mean for it to. It just did. He filled a space I didn't know I'd left vacant. And I was so starved for connection that I fed off of his energy, his compliments, his hunger for me. It felt good…until it didn't.

What I didn't know was that RG wasn't just falling in love; he was falling into obsession.

At first, it was small things. Showing up unannounced. Asking questions about my schedule. He wanted to know more than I was comfortable sharing. But I brushed it off. Told myself he was just being protective. Just interested.

But it turned dark when I tried to pull away. I thought we could go our separate ways quietly with no drama and no mess. I was wrong. He started showing up at places he had no business being. One day, during a showing of the house we were trying to rent, he appeared out of nowhere. Smiling. Charming. Walking the property like he was just another interested renter. But I knew better. I could feel the storm in his smile.

Then came the day I almost died. I got in my car and started driving like normal. I hadn't gone far before something felt wrong. The brakes have just gone. I was coming up fast on a storefront, and I swerved hard, barely avoiding a crash into the Napa Auto building. Heart pounding, I sat in the car, shaking. I didn't know what had happened, but deep down, I knew who had made it happen.

RG later admitted it. Said it plainly, like it wasn't the most terrifying thing I'd ever heard: *"If I can't have you, nobody will."* He threatened to tell my husband. He dangled the secret like a knife and smiled while twisting it.

The strap he wore? That wasn't just fashion, it was a warning. I saw it too late.

What scared me the most wasn't just the car, the threat, or the look in his eyes. It was the realization that I had let this man into my life. I had opened the door, handed him a key, and now he wouldn't leave. He was following my sister. Showing up at my mother's house. Calling my aunt. My mess had spilled over and was drowning my family.

I later found out he had a past I never could have imagined. He had once thrown his ex-wife out of a window for cheating on him. A whole wife. A whole human being. And now he was in my life. How close had I come to being her?

I felt sick. And I felt guilty for letting it get that far, for being reckless, for underestimating the depth of someone else's darkness. But the fear? That part never left me.

I started waking up screaming in the middle of the night. My husband would shake me and ask what was wrong. I couldn't even speak. What could I say? That I was afraid the man I brought into my world might kill me? That the affair I thought was a secret had nearly ended my life?

I kept it inside. I held it close like a secret grenade, hoping it wouldn't go off. The strangest part was that in the middle of all this, my husband still had no clue. He was still cheating, still distant. I should've left. I should've run.

But I stayed. Because of my children. Because I couldn't stomach the idea of a broken home. I had come from that; I knew what it felt like to watch your family crumble. I didn't want that for my babies. I wanted to preserve some version of normal, even if it was built on silence, lies, and fear.

Survival is a powerful thing. It'll make you stay when everything inside you is screaming to go. It'll make you smile when your spirit is weeping. It'll make you lie to yourself to get through the day. That's what I did. For months. For years. I survived.

Eventually, RG moved away. His mother came and got him after I reached out to someone in his family. I never told my husband what happened. Never told him it was RG who cut the brake line. Who stalked me, who whispered death into my ear with the smile of a man who claimed he loved me. When RG left, peace slowly returned. But the damage was already done. I wasn't the same.

I started having more affairs. Not out of lust or love, but numbness. I was broken. I was coping. I was craving a connection that didn't hurt. But all I found were new versions of the same pain. Temporary comfort and long-term chaos.

My marriage limped forward. My heart did not. Even now, there are moments where I look back and wonder how

I survived it. How I didn't become another headline. Another statistic. But only God must have stood between me and the grave that man tried to dig for me.

It's hard to talk about this chapter of my life. Not because I'm ashamed, but because it was so layered in trauma, in survival, and craving. I wasn't chasing destruction. I was chasing escape. And I ran straight into a man who wanted control of my body, my choices, my freedom, and my life.

There's a difference between someone loving you and someone wanting to possess you. I know that now. Love doesn't threaten. It doesn't destroy. It doesn't leave you breathless in fear.

And maybe back then, I didn't know what real love was. But I learned what it wasn't. That affair almost cost me everything. My safety, my sanity, and my life.

But in the end, it gave me something else. Clarity.

The next chapters of my life didn't come smoothly. They came through tears, counselling, and more hard lessons. But I began to see that survival wasn't enough. I didn't want to just make it, I wanted to live. Really live.

And to do that, I had to stop letting broken people define my worth. I had to stop handing out access to people who didn't deserve it.

I had to heal. And I had to forgive myself for the pain I allowed, for the mistakes I made, and for all the times I confused confusion for love.

Pause & Reflect:

Has your intuition ever warned you about a situation or person? Did you listen?

CHAPTER 7: EMPTY HANDS & FULL FAITH

"When you lost everything, you found Me. That was never an accident."

There comes a point in every woman's life where she chooses between surviving in pieces or stepping out into the mysterious in hopes of finding peace. I had reached that point with nothing but a pair of keys in my hand and the weight of every broken promise. I wasn't running away, I was finally walking toward myself.

The second affair in my life was born out of pain. When it happened, I wasn't looking for love. I wasn't even looking for companionship. I was looking for relief from the numbness, from the betrayal, and from the years of being silenced in my own home. I had spent so long pretending that everything was okay that I didn't recognize myself anymore. The affair was a mask I put on to cope, a way to tell myself I still had control, when deep down I was extrication. I knew it wasn't right, but in the moment, it felt like something was better than nothing.

There was a kind of rage simmering inside of me, not the loud, dramatic kind that breaks dishes and punches walls, but the quiet kind that erodes you slowly. I was angry at myself, at the choices I made, at the way I had allowed my worth to be dictated by how someone else treated me. I was angry that love always seemed to come at the cost of my stability.

But more than anything, I was tired. Tired of being treated like an option. Tired of only being welcomed when it was convenient for him. Tired of knocking on a door I once had keys to, reduced to a visitor in a home I helped build. There were nights when I'd stand outside that door, ringing the bell, hoping he'd let me in to see our children, only to be let in when it served his purpose. If he wanted intimacy or needed help, suddenly I was welcome. But if I just wanted to be heard, to be seen, to be valued, I only got the silence.

That wasn't marriage. That was prison with pretty curtains. So, one day, I walked out with nothing but my car keys. No suitcase. No backup plans. No idea what tomorrow looked like.

Just empty hands… and full faith.

I remember gripping that steering wheel like it was the last anchor I had to this earth. My heartbeat was so hard I thought it would crack my ribs. But I kept driving away from the version of myself that had settled. I was leaving behind the woman who tolerated being a placeholder, who silenced her voice to keep peace, who convinced herself that survival was enough.

I didn't have much, but I had something he couldn't take, a will to start over.

I moved in with my mom, and for the first time in years, I had to sit with the silence of my life. No chaos. No manipulation. Just me and the mess I had to clean up. The house was small and full of reminders of where I started, but strangely, it felt safe. It felt like a womb, a place of beginning again.

The days blurred together as I tried to figure out who I was without him. I had built my identity around being his wife, my kids' mother, the fixer of everything broken. But now? I was just Capricia. And I didn't know what that meant yet.

It was around this time, when the weight of my decisions felt unbearable, that I heard the whisper. Not a voice. Not thunder. Just a nudge so deep in my spirit that I knew it wasn't mine.

I had been driving around, looking for somewhere to live, pulling into an apartment complex that looked like every other low-income building I'd grown up near. I was tired, defeated, and honestly? I was about to settle again.

But then I heard it. *"No. Turn around. Go find your car."*

It didn't make sense. I was already in my car. But the message was clear. *"This isn't it. This isn't your home. This isn't your future."*

It was God. I knew it as sure as I knew my name. He was telling me, in His quiet way, *"Daughter, don't go back to the familiar just because it's easier. You've already survived too much to end up back in what you escaped."* That whisper saved me.

It redirected me from making yet another decision out of fear and led me toward trusting the unseen. I drove away from that place with tears in my eyes. Not because I was sad, but because for the first time in a long time, I felt seen. I felt like God hadn't forgotten me, even when I had forgotten myself.

That was the moment everything shifted. I stopped looking for love in empty places and started filling the empty places in me with love.

I stopped needing validation from broken men and started rebuilding my self-worth with bricks of truth. Truth like: "*I am enough. I am worthy. I am not disposable.*"

I knew I had a long road ahead. I was still broke, still emotionally drained, still unsure of what the next step was. But what I did have faith, the only thing I truly needed to begin again.

From that moment on, I made a vow. No more doing things out of anger or desperation. No more tolerating disrespect and calling it love. No more watering dead plants hoping they'd bloom.

I was ready to build a new life. One rooted in real healing, in real faith, in me.

There were days when the fear returned. Nights when I'd sit in the car, crying behind the wheel, asking God how I'd make it, how I'd feed my kids, how I'd pay rent. But I never turned back. Not once. Because even with empty hands, I had something far more powerful:

A whisper from heaven. And that whisper became my compass.

I didn't know it then, but that was the beginning of my climb. From that moment, every tear, every sacrifice, every step forward, even when it felt like crawling, was laying the foundation for a future I couldn't yet see.

But I believed. Even when I had nothing, I believed.

Because sometimes, that's all it takes, a single decision to trust God more than your circumstances. To walk away from what's breaking you.

To leave with nothing but your car keys and your courage. And to listen… for the whisper!

Pause & Reflect:

When was a time you had nothing left — but still found the strength to move forward?

CHAPTER 8: THE WHISPER THAT BUILT AN EMPIRE

"You thought you needed money. I gave you My Word — and that was enough."

I'll never forget that whisper.

It wasn't loud. It wasn't even something you could hear with your ears; it came from deep within, like a pull straight from heaven. It was God. There's no doubt in my mind about that. I didn't have a job. I didn't have money. But I had a whisper, and I had faith.

I had promised myself and my kids that I would never take them backward. I wasn't going to let them live through the pain I came out of. I didn't want them to know that kind of struggle, that kind of brokenness. So even with empty hands, I kept pushing for more. For them. For me. For the life we all deserved.

At one point, I was staying in a cramped two-bedroom home with my extended family, and my three kids squeezed into a space that wasn't meant for us. I had left my old apartment and was trying to figure out what was next. And then it came, that quiet voice. It told me to go look for an apartment.

So, I asked my sister to come with me. We drove around, checking out a few spots, but something didn't fit right. I kept thinking, *"I can't go backward. I can't circle back to where I started."* The next day, that whisper got louder. It told me, *"Go find your car."*

A car? With no job? No steady income?

Yes. A car. That whisper was clear. I needed a way to move around, to go get what was meant for me. I couldn't keep asking people for rides. I couldn't keep waiting on the world to hand me anything. So, I followed that whisper and got myself a car.

Not long after that, I landed a part-time job. And then… I got my house back.

My house, the one I bought before, the one I thought I had lost, it was still mine. I couldn't believe it. That moment, stepping back into something I had once claimed and thought was gone, it felt like renewal. Like God giving me back what the enemy tried to steal. I was the first grandchild in my family to buy a home. That had meant everything to me the first time. And getting it back? That felt even bigger.

That house became my sanctuary. It was where I started to rebuild not just my life, but myself.

I started focusing more on school. I dove back into my business. I start putting the broken pieces of myself back together, piece by piece. I was falling in love with the woman I was becoming. And this time, no one was coming in to interrupt my healing. No one was there to block what God was doing in me. Then came the $65,000 check.

When I saw that number, I didn't scream. I cried. Because I knew it was God. That money didn't just represent a financial breakthrough; it was spiritual confirmation. It was like heaven saying, *"You're on the right path, baby girl. Keep walking."*

I wept tears of joy. All those moments of uncertainty, all the silent prayers, all the nights wondering how I would feed my kids, this was proof that He was listening to me whole time. That whisper wasn't just in my head. It was divine direction.

But even with all that momentum, one fear still gripped me deep: quitting my job.

I had to leave my job to work for myself. And even though I'd already been through so much, that leap into full-time entrepreneurship was terrifying. All my life, I had been taught the American way: you go to school, you graduate, you get a steady job, and you work until retirement. That's what stability looked like. But I chose a different path.

Leaving behind that security wasn't easy. I didn't know if I could make it. But I couldn't keep working someone else's dream while mine sat in the dark. I had to trust the whisper again.

That transition was no joke. People think being your boss means freedom and luxury. Let me tell you, freedom comes with a price. I had to pay for my insurance, maintenance, and every single overhead cost. My gross income wasn't mine once everything was taken out. And the weight of being responsible for others? Whew.

I used to get so mad when jobs wouldn't let me take my vacation days. *"Why I gotta ask you to take time off that I earned?"* I'd grumble. But once I became the boss, and my employees started requesting vacation days during our busiest season, I got it. It finally clicked. If everyone leaves, who's doing the work?

Rules and regulations suddenly made sense. I had a whole new level of respect for every employer I ever had. Running a business was about making decisions, taking hits, and still keeping things afloat.

But let's talk about the money, since everybody loves to ask. With my Airbnb business alone, I now bring in about $30,000 a month. And during tax season? The first three to four months of the year, I pull in close to $100,000 a week.

Yeah. You read that right. A hundred thousand a week.

That's not even including what I make from my rental properties or other ventures. That's just my tax business during peak season. But it didn't happen overnight. It took obedience. It took grit. It took listening to that whisper when I had no job, no car, no house, and no money.

It took saying yes to the hidden. I didn't mention these numbers to brag; I mentioned them because I want you to know what's possible. I built this empire from the ground up, with nothing but faith, determination, and a whisper that refused to leave me alone.

I don't have it all figured out. I still face challenges. But I'm no longer the woman who was stuck in survival mode. I'm the woman who dared to believe God's whisper over the world's noise. And look at me now.

I own my time. I own my peace. I own my purpose. And it all started with a whisper!

Pause & Reflect:

What quiet inner voice or dream have you been ignoring, and what would happen if you trusted it?

CHAPTER 9: FROM PROJECTS TO PENTHOUSE

"Every brick you laid was a prayer, I had already answered. You just had to walk it out."

If someone had told me back in the projects that I'd one day own multiple businesses, drive the car of my dreams, and live in a gated community where celebrities were my neighbours. I might have smiled politely, but I wouldn't have believed it.

I knew I was made for more, but I didn't yet know how to get there. What I didn't realize then was that the path from poverty to prosperity wasn't going to be a straight line. It would be built brick by brick, sometimes painfully, from trial, faith, setbacks, and sacrifice.

My first attempt at entrepreneurship was shaky. I had the vision, but the partnership wasn't right. My husband at the time had the skill set to do tech services, but he lacked the drive to charge for his work. He was more interested in doing favours for friends than building something sustainable.

We had a few clients, but it was like pulling teeth to get him to treat it like a real business. And when I brought up the idea of starting a tax office, he laughed on my face. *"Who is going to pay for it?"* he asked. I had done my research. I knew it didn't take much to get started. But instead of support, I got resistance.

Still, I had already started dabbling in travel before taxes. Booking flights for friends and acquaintances, I made a little money here and there. It wasn't enough, but it showed me what was possible. So, when the door slammed shut on the tech business, I pushed open a window into taxes. After my husband and I separated, I went full speed ahead. I started small by just helping family: cousins, aunties, and in-laws. Word spread. They referred people, and soon, I had built a small but growing business.

I turned the den in my house into a makeshift tax office. I networked. I handed out cards. I helped people get their refunds when they were stuck or couldn't reach the IRS. I earned trust, one return at a time. And before I knew it, I had over 300 clients in one season. I was doing taxes on my lunch break at work, between classes at school, and late at night while everyone else slept.

Then COVID hit. That was the turning point. More people needed help, and I started hiring, just a few employees at first. We worked out of my home, but that quickly became dangerous. When the government sent out stimulus checks to the last known deposit account (often the tax office's intermediary account), people didn't understand the process. They showed up at my house banging on the door, accusing me of stealing their money. I knew then it was time to get a professional office.

I prayed. And that same voice I'd always heard the one that had guided me since childhood, spoke again. *"Drive around. Look."* I obeyed. Every place I checked felt wrong, until I found a 1,200-square-foot space that was perfect. The landlord offered it for $1,000 a month, no penalties, and no strings. I didn't even have furniture yet, but I took it. I hustled. Found desks and reception furniture on Facebook Marketplace, pieced everything together with love and faith.

The first year in that storefront, it was just me and one employee. That season, we made over $600,000, just the two of us. I didn't spend recklessly. I didn't travel. I didn't shop. I saved. The next season, I scaled. Hired more people. We made over a million dollars in three months. That's when it hit me, I was a real entrepreneur. A multimillionaire. From the projects to penthouse, quite literally.

Once that seed took root, I kept planting.

My boyfriend suggested we start a courier service. He was making $2,000–$3,000 a day delivering for a popular beverage brand and other companies. I supported him, and eventually, I went back to school to become a freight broker so I could help on the backend. More income. More independence.

Then my daughter came to me with an idea: a hair business, bundles, wigs, and products. I loved it. My sister got excited too and came up with a name, Garden of Weave. I was ready to collaborate, but she moved slowly, and I couldn't wait. I started the business to support my daughter's vision. It did well, but it sparked tension. My sister felt excluded. I didn't mean to hurt her, but I also knew I couldn't slow my pace to match someone else's procrastination. That lesson was bitter: not everyone wants success at the same speed you do.

In time, I bought my dream home in an exclusive neighbourhood—, but I held onto my old house. That house held history. I remodelled it and turned it into an Airbnb. It was booked constantly. Then I bought another house. And another. I began renting to insurance companies that placed displaced families after disasters. One home brought in

$94,000 over 15 months. Another made $40,000 in just nine months. My passive income grew without me having to punch a clock. My Airbnb's averaged $2,000 a month. I had done it. I had built an empire.

But money doesn't erase problems, it magnifies them.

I struggled with what I now know is survivor's remorse. I felt like I owed people because I made it out. I tried to help everyone, I gave money, created jobs, opened doors, but it backfired. Family started to feel entitled. They acted like they were owed a piece of my pie just because we shared DNA. I tried to build with them, but many didn't have the discipline or the respect to match my effort. One of my sisters almost ruined my tax business with how she treated clients, cussing them out, being rude, and acting like she owned the place. I had to let her go.

Others, instead of saying thank you, gossiped and twisted the truth. Two of my sisters began speaking badly about me to my fiancé at the time. Told him how much money I had. Stirred up jealousy. I never flaunted my success, but once they told him I was a millionaire, his demeanour changed.

He started pulling away, cheating. Some men don't know how to handle a successful woman. I did my best to uplift him, but you can't dim your light to make someone else comfortable in your glow.

It hurt deeply. I felt betrayed, not just by him, but by my own blood. People I had trusted. Helped. Fed. Paid. People I thought would cheer for me turned on me. I learned to keep quiet. These days, if someone asks me about my plans or how I'm doing, I just smile. I've learned not to offer information unless it's asked for, and even then, I give only what's necessary.

The only thing that kept me grounded through all of this was God.

I prayed. Constantly. When I didn't know what to do, I listened to that still small voice. Sometimes I ignored it, and I paid the price. Now I know better. When the voice says, *"Be quiet,"* I stay quiet. When it says, *"Let them go,"* I don't hold on. When it says, *"Move,"* I move.

I don't argue. I don't beg. I don't explain. I just follow the path God has for me.

I've stopped trying to be the fixer for everyone else's problems. I support when I can, but I don't sacrifice my peace for anyone's approval anymore. And as I continue to build, I do so with full faith, an open heart, and a firm boundary.

From the projects to the penthouse was about mindset. It was about learning that I was worthy of success, even when others couldn't handle it. It was about surviving, more than that, it was about becoming.

And I'm still becoming. Every day.

Pause & Reflect:

What is your definition of success, and are you building toward it or away from it?

CHAPTER 10: CHEMO, CHRIST, & COURAGE

"The sickness didn't come to kill you. It came to reveal the warrior I made you to be."

I still remember the way the word cancer landed in the room, as if the air got sucked out and everything stood silent. I didn't hear anything else the doctor said after breast cancer. My ears rang, my hands trembled, and my vision blurred as tears streamed down my face. I thought it was the end. After everything I'd survived, after all the mountains I had climbed, it felt like this was where my story would stop. I cried like a child.

For a brief moment, I honestly believed I had reached my limit. My body had taken so many hits in life, abuse, heartbreak, betrayal, survival, and now this. Cancer. I whispered to God in the quiet of my bedroom that night, *"Is this really it?"* And clear as day, I heard Him speak to my spirit. One thing I've always known about God is this: He prepares you for the storm long before you see the clouds coming.

I didn't know it at the time, but He had already set my path straight before cancer ever touched my body. See, I didn't even know if I still had insurance. After my divorce, I assumed my ex-husband had removed me from his plan. But in a moment that I can only call divine, I found out I was still covered. When I called Kaiser, the woman on the phone said, *"Ma'am, you're still on his insurance."* I couldn't believe it. He never dropped me, even without realizing it. And when he found out I had cancer, he said, *"If I had known, I never would've taken you off."* But God already made sure I didn't fall through the cracks. He had me covered, literally.

Because of that divine coverage, I was able to go through chemo and radiation without the crushing burden of medical debt. I didn't have to worry about scraping together thousands of dollars to stay alive. God knew I needed every bit of my strength to fight, so He handled the rest.

And as if that wasn't enough, He made sure my life stayed afloat. I was able to keep paying my mortgage, even on my brand-new home. I managed to pay both leases on my two offices after expanding the business. I paid my employees, kept the lights on, kept food on the table, and didn't miss a single car note. The numbers didn't make sense on paper, but somehow it all worked. That was nothing but God, no math, no formula, just divine provision.

Business didn't stop, even when my body wanted to. Everything kept moving. My companies, though hit by inflation, tariffs, and slowdowns, still pulled in over a million dollars. Even with setbacks from betrayal and stolen clientele, my businesses survived. God never let me fall too far. Some things dipped, like travel and courier services, but other streams stayed steady. What God gave me, no man could steal. Even when it looked like everything might crumble, He whispered, *"You will stand."*

But let me be honest, chemo didn't care about my faith, my title, or my bank account. It was brutal. I lost strength, I lost sleep, and for a moment, I almost lost my life.

There was a night I'll never forget. My body was failing in ways that terrified me. I kept going to the doctor, but no one could figure out what was wrong. My sisters and husband, one of the few who stood by me through it, kept driving me back and forth, desperate for answers. My husband at the time was doing all he could, but still, we were getting nowhere. And then something inside me said, *"Go to Piedmont."*

I told my sister, *"Take me to Piedmont Hospital."*

The minute I arrived, they finally discovered what was going on. I had developed sepsis. My chemo port was infected, and I was dangerously close to death. They admitted me immediately. I underwent surgery after surgery, some of them without anaesthesia because of how severe things had gotten. The pain? It was indescribable. I'd faced so many kinds of pain in life, emotional, mental, even spiritual, but this was different. This was the kind of pain that tested my will to live.

And still, I clung to life. I clung to my faith.

Even in that hospital bed, even when I was being cut open wide awake, I refused to let fear win. I heard a whisper in my ear that said, *"Fear means death."* It was more than just a voice; it was the truth. If I gave in to fear, I was going to die. But if I stood in faith, I'd live.

So, I chose life. I chose faith.

And when that same whisper told me, *"Faith means life,"* I started speaking it over myself daily. Life. Life. Life. I spoke it when my body was breaking. I spoke it when the betrayal of family members cut deeper than any surgeon's knife. I spoke it when clients were stolen, and my heart ached from the loss. Life.

I believe in the power of the tongue. Always have. That's why I guarded my energy fiercely. During chemo, I couldn't handle negativity. I couldn't afford to entertain gossip, complaints, or toxic people. I told folks straight up, *"I can't talk right now,"* or *"I'll call you back,"* and sometimes I just let the phone ring. I had to protect my peace like my life depended on it, because it did.

My daughters, my sons, and a few loyal employees stepped up when I physically couldn't. I leaned on them. I delegated. I let go of trying to control every little thing. I had to. There were moments I felt deeply abandoned, especially by one of my sisters, who I thought would have my back. She quit on me, right when I needed her most, and told lies about me on top of it. That betrayal stung more than chemo. Because I would've done anything for her, I had done everything for her. But when it was my turn to lean on her, she let me fall. That broke something in me. But even then, I didn't let bitterness take root.

I kept walking.

I kept believing.

This chapter of my life reminded me that real strength isn't loud. It's not always visible. Sometimes it looks like dragging yourself out of bed just to sit in a chair. Sometimes it's the silent prayers in the middle of the night or the tears you cry when no one's looking. Courage doesn't always roar. Sometimes, it whispers, *"I'll try again tomorrow."*

Through cancer, I found a deeper version of myself. A woman refined by fire, not destroyed by it. A mother, a fighter, a believer. Chemo tried to break me, but Christ rebuilt me.

And now, standing on the other side of it, I can say with boldness: cancer didn't win. I did. Not because I'm superhuman, but because I serve a supernatural God.

Pause & Reflect

What did hardship teach you about faith, and how did it change the way you live or lead?

CHAPTER 11: FAMILY, FAITH, & FRACTURES

"Not every bond is meant to stay whole — I break what burdens you, even if it bleeds."

Motherhood didn't just change my life, it saved it.

There were so many moments when I could've lost myself completely, when the pain I carried felt like too much weight for one woman to hold. But then I'd hear the sound of little feet running down the hallway or catch my baby's eyes staring up at me like I was her entire world, and suddenly, I remembered I had more than myself to live for.

My children gave me a reason to stay grounded. They gave my chaos a purpose. And they reminded me, day after day, that the cycle had to stop with me. I didn't have the luxury to fall apart, not when they were watching. Not when their idea of strength, of womanhood, of God... was all being shaped through me.

In their eyes, I became something more than human. I became shelter. I became home. I became love. And though I was none of those things for myself at the time, I tried to be them for my children.

Even in the middle of my brokenness, I held myself together because I knew they were looking at me like I was invincible. And sometimes? That was the only thing that kept me from doing something reckless. The only thing that pulled me back from the edge.

But being a mother, especially a single mother, and an entrepreneur, came with battles that nobody warned me about.

The hardest part wasn't just the sleepless nights or the bills stacking up. It was the emotional toll of trying to protect their innocence when the world kept trying to take it. I worked so hard to keep the ugliness of my past, the darkness of my surroundings, and the messiness of adult life from touching their little hearts. But some of it still slipped through the cracks.

There's only so much you can shield them from. Life has a way of leaking through the walls, no matter how hard you patch them. And I had to come to terms with the fact that I couldn't save them from everything. I could only prepare them. love them fiercely, lead them with integrity, and hope that my strength would become their foundation.

One of the biggest lessons I tried to teach them was self-love. Because I didn't grow up with much of it. And I knew first-hand what it cost to walk through life not knowing your worth.

But while I was raising them to be whole, I was also trying to hold the pieces of myself together. And at the same time. I was breaking in other areas of my life.

No one talks about how success can strain the very relationships you hoped it would heal. You think that once you "make it," once you build something real, your people will be proud. They'll celebrate you. They'll finally see how hard you worked. But sometimes, that's not how it plays out.

Sometimes the more you rise, the more fractured things become.

That's what happened with me and my siblings.

I don't want to throw the word jealousy around, because they swore it wasn't that. But it felt like hate. It felt like resentment, the kind that builds when people can't understand how you managed to do what they couldn't, even though they watched you struggle.

I poured into them. Gave them time, money, opportunity, and mentorship. Everything I wished someone had given me. But still, it was never enough.

They started getting mad if I went somewhere and didn't tell them. Mad if I took one sister out and not the other. If I did something and didn't invite everyone, it became a whole scene. And before long, it was like I couldn't breathe without someone twisting my words or taking offense to something I never even said.

It felt like I was under surveillance, like I was always one step away from being cancelled by my own blood.

Maybe they wanted my attention. Maybe they wanted to know the secret to how I did it. But the truth is, there is no secret. Just sacrifice. Lots of it. Sacrifices that they didn't see and maybe weren't willing to make themselves.

They wanted the glow but not the grind. The shine but not the scars.

What hurt most was not the friction, it was the fact that I kept trying to prove I was still me. Still Capricia. Still the sister who would give you the shirt off her back. But no matter how much I gave, it wasn't enough to fill whatever void they were projecting onto me.

At some point, I had to stop trying to fix it.

I had to accept that not everyone is meant to come with you to every level. Even family. Even people you love with your whole heart.

That was one of the hardest pills to swallow. Because deep down, I always thought, *"If I win, we all win."* But not everyone saw it that way.

Still, I kept going. Not out of pride, but out of purpose.

Because the same God that walked me through the fire, walked me through those fractures. And in those quiet, painful moments when I didn't have the words or the strength to explain myself, I remembered the words my grandmother used to say: ***"You are blessed and highly favoured."***

That phrase wasn't just something sweet she'd say when things were good. She said it when we had nothing. When we were struggling. When I was crying and broken and trying to figure out why life had to be so hard. She said it like it was a promise, one that couldn't be shaken by circumstance.

Now, years later, I carry that same phrase like armour. I say it aloud to remind myself that I'm not here by luck. I'm here by divine appointment. I'm here because I'm blessed and highly favoured, even when it doesn't feel like it.

Even when my own blood turns cold.

Even when the world doesn't clap.

Even when I'm doing it alone.

Because if you only knew the things I've survived, the things I haven't even told yet, you'd understand that it's nothing short of a miracle that I'm still standing.

And every miracle has a cost.

Sometimes that cost is comfort. Sometimes it's connection. But always, it's calling you higher.

I may not have done everything right. I've made mistakes, plenty of them. But what I've never done is give up. And I've never stopped loving the people God gave me, even when they couldn't see the love behind my actions.

Motherhood taught me to be selfless.

Entrepreneurship taught me to be fearless.

Fractured relationships taught me to be resilient.

And my faith? My faith taught me that no matter what breaks, God can rebuild it. Even me!

Pause & Reflect:

Where do you need to set a boundary to protect your peace, even if it's painful?

CHAPTER 12: BROKEN TO BLESSED

"Your scars are holy; Your story is sacred. And your blessing was always on the way."

There's a light at the end of every tunnel, even the ones we can't see when we're in them.

If there's one thing I hope is never forgotten about my story, it's that simple truth. No matter how far gone things feel, no matter how heavy the struggle, there is always a breakthrough waiting, usually when we're just about ready to give up. We live in a world that pushes urgency. But growth doesn't come from rushing. It comes from waiting. From breathing. From letting the storm pass before making a move.

Every time I waited, even when I was angry, hurt, or felt like reacting, that's when the real answers came. Patience has always been my greatest breakthrough. It saved me from making decisions I couldn't take back. It taught me to stop, wait, and let God speak before I did.

The losses, they came like waves. But each wave pulled something out of me, and left something stronger in its place. I used to think loss meant something had been taken from me. Now I know better. What I lost wasn't for me. Every single thing I thought I needed, every person who left, every opportunity that slipped through my fingers, those weren't failures. They were protection. Refinement. If I had kept all that I once cried over, I wouldn't have made it to this moment. Some things would've broken me. Some people would've kept me small.

Instead, loss became my blessing. My maturity came through grief. My strength was shaped in silence. And with every single thing I lost, God gave it back to me a thousand times over.

There was a time when I had a completely different picture of what success looked like. I thought it meant having money, owning things, and being admired. But now I know real success is peace. It's discipline. It's clarity. It's knowing who you are and refusing to shrink for anyone.

The path to that kind of success required a complete mindset shift. I had to let go of toxic environments, negative thinking, and people who weren't walking in the same direction. You can't keep holding on to dead weight and expect to rise. When I changed my mind, I changed my life. I replaced fear with focus. I replaced bad company with purpose-filled people. That's when things started unlocking for me. Doors opened. Strategies aligned. Patience became power.

Now I move differently. I don't chase. I don't force. I flow with what's meant for me. And when something doesn't align, when a step feels off or the road gets bumpy, I stop. That's how I know it's not God. Because He's not the author of confusion. He's not going to bless anything that isn't meant for me. And He definitely won't give me something I'm not mature enough to handle.

There were years when I wished for wealth. But I know now, if He had given it to me back then, I would've wasted it all. My mindset wasn't ready. My heart wasn't steady. I would've spent it on things that don't last, cars, shoes, houses, and been right back at zero. Now, I've grown into someone who can not only receive the blessing but also sustain it. I've learned how to make wise choices, how to say no, how to invest, and how to pour back into others without draining myself.

I still have a soft spot for people. That hasn't changed. But now I give with wisdom. I give from overflow, not emptiness. That's what maturity looks like for me.

Everything I went through, every dark corner, every lonely night, every battle with sickness, poverty, shame, it wasn't just for me. I know God carried me through it all for a reason. These weren't just tests. They were testimonies in the making. And now, I carry them not as scars, but as keys. Keys that might unlock someone else's cage. I know there are people walking through the same fire I once did. And some of them don't know if they'll make it. But maybe, just maybe, my story can help them hold on.

That's why I wrote this book. Not for fame. Not for attention. But to show someone else what survival looks like when it's covered in grace. I believe my life was allowed to go the way it did so I could become a voice, so I could be proof. Because some people aren't strong enough to carry what I carried. Some people are still trying to figure out how to stand back up.

Maybe this story will reach them. Maybe it'll remind someone they're not alone. Maybe it'll catch a woman in the middle of her breakdown and give her just enough hope to keep going. And maybe one day, this story won't just be a book, it'll be a movie. Because I didn't survive just for myself. I survived so others could rise.

And no, I don't want this message to stop at the borders of the U.S. My pain wasn't local, so my purpose can't be either. There are people hurting in Africa, in Dubai, in Thailand, and in every corner of this world. Poverty isn't confined. Trauma doesn't have a zip code. My story may start with brokenness, but it ends with blessing. And that journey, that transformation, it's something the whole world deserves to see.

Because I didn't just go through it. I grew through it.

And now, I'm standing in the blessing I once prayed for, with both feet planted, my heart open, and my hands full.

Pause & Reflect:

What's one scar or failure from your past that is secretly shaping your strength today?

FINAL LETTER FROM AUTHOR

Dear Reader,

If you've made it this far, I want to say: thank you. Not just for reading my story, but for holding space for the pain, the healing, the mess, the miracles, and the moments in between.

I didn't write this book to be admired. I wrote it so **you would know you're not alone**.

To the **woman in an abusive relationship** — I see you. I know how quietly the soul can bleed when your body is still standing. You don't need anyone else's permission to choose yourself. **God will catch you** when you walk — and He'll rebuild what you thought you lost.

To the **teen mom** who feels invisible — I was you. Tired, judged, and buried under responsibility. But I want you to know: **your baby is not your end. It's your beginning.** You are still worthy of love, success, and a life beyond survival.

To the **survivor of childhood trauma** — I know how it feels to carry secrets that aren't yours, to wear shame like skin. But you are not broken. You are **a sacred restoration project** — and healing is your birthright.

To the **dreamer from humble beginnings** — never let anyone tell you you're too "damaged" or too "poor" to build an empire. I went from homeless to millionaire by listening to **a whisper** that the world couldn't hear. And if He did it for me, **He can do it for you.**

Every scar you carry has a name. But so does every victory wait for you on the other side of faith.

Walk boldly. Love yourself completely. And never stop listening for the whisper.

With all my heart,

Capricia A. Sloan

Built from Broken — But never forgotten.

www.ingramcontent.com/pod-product-compliance
Lightning Source LLC
Chambersburg PA
CBHW051331120626
46547CB00016B/2486

* 9 7 8 1 9 6 5 5 5 5 4 5 3 *